FAST Lane
OPEN-WHEEL RACING

FORMULA 1

By Tyrone Georgiou

Gareth Stevens
Publishing

Please visit our website, www.garethstevens.com. For a free color catalog of all our high-quality books, call toll free 1-800-542-2595 or fax 1-877-542-2596.

Library of Congress Cataloging-in-Publication Data

Georgiou, Tyrone.
 Formula 1 / Tyrone Georgiou.
     p. cm. — (Fast lane, open-wheel racing)
 Includes index.
 ISBN 978-1-4339-5752-9 (pbk.)
 ISBN 978-1-4339-5753-6 (6-pack)
 ISBN 978-1-4339-5750-5 (lib. bdg.)
 1. Automobile racing—Juvenile literature. 2. Automobiles, Racing—Juvenile literature. 3. Formula One automobiles—Juvenile literature. I. Title. II. Title: Formula one.
 GV1029.13.G46 2011
 796.72—dc22

                                    2010050933

First Edition

Published in 2012 by
Gareth Stevens Publishing
111 East 14th Street, Suite 349
New York, NY 10003

Copyright © 2012 Gareth Stevens Publishing

Designer: Daniel Hosek
Editor: Greg Roza

Photo credits: Cover, p. 1 Shutterstock.com; pp. 4–5 (main image) Andrew Hone/Getty Images; p. 5 (fast fact) Shaun Botterill/Getty Images; pp. 6–7 (main image) Clive Mason/Getty Images; p. 7 (fast fact) Tony Duffy/Getty Images; p. 9 Lipnitzki/Roger Viollet/Getty Images; p. 11 (main image) Steve Powell/Getty Images; p. 11 (fast fact) Central Press/Hulton Archive/Getty Images; p. 13 (main image) Fred Dufour/AFP/Getty Images; p. 13 (fast fact) Gabriel Bouys/AFP/Getty Images; p. 15 (main image) Pascal Rondeau/Getty Images; p. 15 (fast fact) Stuart Franklin/Bongarts/Getty Images; p. 17 (main image) AFP/Getty Images; p. 17 (fast fact) Peter Parks/AFP/Getty Images; p. 19 (main image) Mauricio Lima/AFP/Getty Images; p. 19 (fast fact) Pool/AFP/Getty Images.

Printed in the United States of America

CPSIA compliance information: Batch #CS11GS: For further information contact Gareth Stevens, New York, New York at 1-800-542-2595.

CONTENTS

Words in the glossary appear in **bold** type the first time they are used in the text.

Formula 1 (F1) is the world's top open-wheel racing series. Why is it called "open-wheel"? It's because the wheels stick out beyond the car's body and aren't covered.

The F1 racing season lasts 9 months and includes about 20 races in countries around the world. Drivers battle for the championship while teams try to win the constructor title. Driving skills, **engineering**, **strategy**, and the latest racing **innovations** are the things that make a winning team.

Fast Fact

A Formula 1 team can have only two drivers and two cars, but each team has a staff of several hundred people and its own manufacturing center.

a Formula 1 team's staff

Formula 1 driver Sebastian Vettel races in Abu Dhabi, United Arab Emirates.

5

WHAT'S A FORMULA 1 CAR?

A Formula 1 car isn't like an ordinary car. It's built to a very special set of rules, which change often. In 2011, the rules called for a four-wheel car with a **V-8 engine** and a weight of at least 1,408 pounds (640 kg). Other rules govern the length, width, and height of the car, as well as the features of the tires, engine, fuel tank, and body. Today's F1 cars are manufactured using special **composites** and metal **alloys**.

Fast Fact

In 1976, the Tyrrell-Ford P34 six-wheel GP car won the Swedish Grand Prix. Its four small front wheels produced better braking and handling than two larger wheels.

Coming up with creative answers to special rules is what successful F1 racing is all about.

THE STARTING LINE

Formula 1 racing was originally called Grand Prix racing. It began in the early 1900s when automobiles gained popularity in Europe. Teams from France, Italy, Germany, and other European countries raced on roads between towns instead of on closed tracks like those used today. This age is known as the classic period of formula racing. It ended in 1940 with the start of World War II. The modern Grand Prix era began in 1950, when the first Formula 1 championship was held.

"Grand Prix" is French for "grand prize." Formula 1 racing is often still called Grand Prix racing.

THE GREAT TEAMS

Formula 1 racing has had many great racing teams. Enzo Ferrari led the Italian Alfa Romeo team in the 1930s and 1940s before creating his own famous team in the 1950s. Ferrari has won a record 215 races. The McLaren team of England has the second-best record with 169 wins.

The English Lotus team's race car design led F1 racing throughout the 1960s and 1970s. The English Williams team ruled the 1980s and 1990s with 113 race victories.

Fast Fact

Lotus founder Colin Chapman invented the "ground effect" race car. By shaping the sides of his F1 car like upside-down wings, he greatly improved the car's speed and handling.

Colin Chapman

Colin Chapman (in the black cap) talks with driver Mario Andretti before a race in 1979.

FAMOUS GRAND PRIX TRACKS

Some F1 tracks are as famous as the great teams and drivers. The track in Monte Carlo, Monaco, is a twisting, curving street track. Originally built in the 1920s, the Nürburgring near Nürburg, Germany, was considered the most deadly track in F1. The new track built in 1984 is shorter and safer. Belgium's Spa-Francorchamps track runs through the Ardennes Forest. This high-speed track is the longest in F1. The Monza track is the pride of Italian motor sports.

Fast Fact The last US Grand Prix was run at the famed Indianapolis Motor Speedway in 2007. Cars ran in the opposite direction that cars race during the annual Indianapolis 500 race.

Two Ferrari drivers speed around a corner on the Monaco racetrack in 2009.

13

THE GREATS OF GRAND PRIX

Italian driver Tazio Nuvolari was perhaps the greatest racer of the classic period. He scored 45 wins and one European championship. Juan Manuel Fangio of Argentina was the first driver in modern F1 racing to win multiple world championships. Fangio had 24 wins and five world championships. Jim Clark of Scotland raced lightweight, rear-engine cars for Lotus in the 1960s. Brazilian driver Ayrton Senna was considered one of the most talented racers of all time before he died in a crash in 1994.

Michael Schumacher of Germany has the most F1 wins with 91. He quit racing in 2007. However, in 2010, at the age of 41, he returned to drive for the new Mercedes team.

Michael Schumacher

Ayrton Senna celebrates after winning the 1991 Brazilian Grand Prix.

GRAND PRIX RACING WEEKEND

Formula 1 racing is a 3-day event. Racers practice on day 1. Teams make changes to their cars. Drivers find the best "line" around the track. On day 2, **qualifying sessions** decide how the racers will line up for the race.

Day 3 is race time! Drivers line up in a **grid** based on how they did during the qualifying sessions. They race for about 190 miles (305 km). Each driver tries to come in first and earn points for their team.

Fast Fact

Formula 1 occurs in all types of weather, so there are different tires for different conditions. Picking the right tires can be the difference between winning and crashing.

Racers line up in the grid just before the start of the 2010 Chinese Grand Prix.

17

BETWEEN THE RACES

Getting a Formula 1 team from one race to the next is a huge job. The races are just a few weeks apart, and they're often held on different **continents**! The team has more to move than just the drivers and their cars. It also needs to move mechanics, engineers, and everyone else. Spare parts, tools, and computers are all loaded into specially created carriers, which are then loaded onto a jumbo jet for a trip around the world.

An F1 team has 20 or more mechanics in the **pits** at a race. When a car comes into the pits, all mechanics might work on the car at the same time. This makes the pits a very busy place.

A mechanic for the Ferrari team unloads a carrier of supplies several days before a race.

TODAY'S TOP F1 DRIVERS

Fernando Alonso of Spain races for Ferrari. In 2010, at age 29, Alonso already had 26 wins and two world championships. Alonso has also raced for Renault and McLaren.

England's Lewis Hamilton races for McLaren. By 2010, he had 14 wins and a world championship. Hamilton got his start racing go-karts at the age of 8.

German driver Sebastian Vettel races for Renault. In 2010, he became the youngest world champion ever at age 23.

F1 RACING NUMBERS

Most Total Team Wins	215, Ferrari
Most Driver Wins	269, Michael Schumacher
Most Driver Wins in a Season	13, Michael Schumacher, 2004
Youngest Race Winner	Sebastian Vettel, age 21, 2008 Italian Grand Prix
Youngest World Champion	Sebastian Vettel, age 23, 2010

GLOSSARY

alloy: a mixture of two or more metals, or a metal and nonmetal

composite: a solid made from two or more kinds of matter

continent: one of Earth's seven great landmasses

engineering: the use of science and math to build better objects

grid: the starting positions of cars on a racetrack

innovation: a new invention, or a new way of doing things

pits: a place along the side of a racetrack where cars get fuel and have problems fixed

qualifying session: a driving period before a race used to decide drivers' places on the grid. The results are based on speed.

strategy: a careful plan for winning

V-8 engine: a motor where the two banks of cylinders are arranged in a V shape

22

FOR MORE INFORMATION

Books

Mason, Paul. *Formula 1*. Mankato, MN: Amicus, 2011.

Von Finn, Denny. *Formula 1 Cars*. Minneapolis, MN: Bellwether Media, 2010.

Websites

Formula 1

www.formula1.com
Visit the official website of Formula 1 racing to read about recent events, rules, history, and more.

Planet F1

www.planetf1.com
Read more about Formula 1 racing.

INDEX